this OR that?
weather

tidal wave OR tsunami?

Kelly Doudna

Consulting Editor, Diane Craig, M.A./Reading Specialist

Super Sandcastle

An Imprint of Abdo Publishing
abdopublishing.com

abdopublishing.com

Printed in the United States of America, North Mankato, Minnesota

102015

012016

 THIS BOOK CONTAINS RECYCLED MATERIALS

Editor: Liz Salzmann
Content Developer: Nancy Tuminelly
Cover and Interior Design and Production: Mighty Media, Inc.
Photo Credits: Kelly Doudna, NOAA, Shutterstock, Wikimedia

Library of Congress Cataloging-in-Publication Data

Doudna, Kelly, 1963- author.
  Tidal wave or tsunami? / Kelly Doudna ; consulting editor, Diane Craig.
    pages cm -- (This or that? Weather)
  ISBN 978-1-62403-956-0
1. Tsunamis--Juvenile literature. I. Craig, Diane, editor. II. Title.
  GC221.5.D65 2016
  551.46'37--dc23
                    2015021246

Super SandCastle™ books are created by a team of professional educators, reading specialists, and content developers around five essential components—phonemic awareness, phonics, vocabulary, text comprehension, and fluency—to assist young readers as they develop reading skills and strategies and increase their general knowledge. All books are written, reviewed, and leveled for guided reading and early reading intervention programs for use in shared, guided, and independent reading and writing activities to support a balanced approach to literacy instruction.

contents

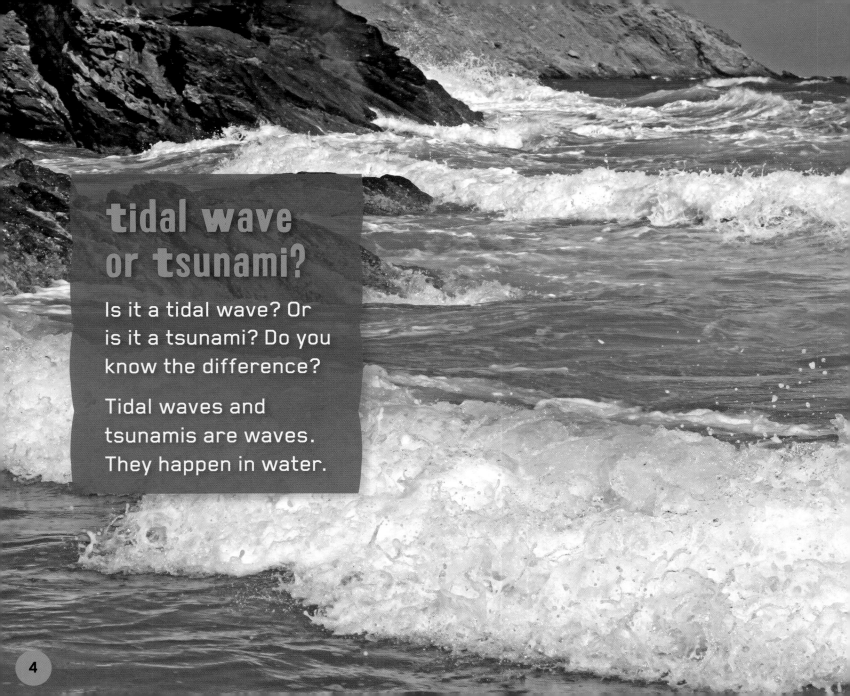

tidal wave or tsunami?

Is it a tidal wave? Or is it a tsunami? Do you know the difference?

Tidal waves and tsunamis are waves. They happen in water.

Tsunamis and tidal waves are different kinds of waves. Tsunamis are larger than tidal waves.

where they happen

Tidal waves and tsunamis happen in large bodies of water. Tidal waves occur in the ocean.

Most tsunamis happen in the ocean. But they can also form in large lakes.

what is the tide?

Tidal waves are caused by the ocean tide. The moon and the sun pull on the oceans. This causes the oceans to swell. The thick parts line up with the moon. This is the tide.

The tide seems to move. But it doesn't. It stays lined up with the moon. The earth turns beneath the swell.

pull of sun's gravity

pull of moon's gravity

moon

sun

gravity causes oceans to bulge in direction of pull

sun and moon's gravity pull together

The tide is a **cycle**. It has high water. Then it has low water. The tide comes in. It raises the water level along the coast. The tide goes out. The water level falls again.

A tidal bore is a kind of tidal wave. The tide goes into a narrow space, such as a river. The land acts like a funnel. The tide forces the water into a wave. This is a tidal bore.

a bunch of waves

Movement of land under the water starts a tsunami. An **earthquake** or a **landslide** can cause the land to move. The sudden movement pushes the water. It forms waves.

A tsunami can have many waves.
They follow each other.

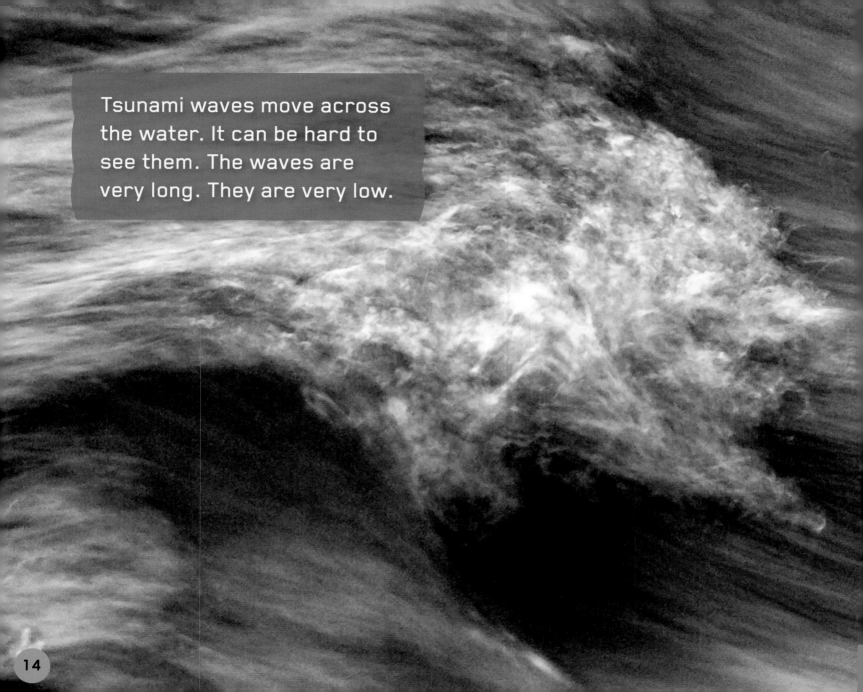

Tsunami waves move across the water. It can be hard to see them. The waves are very long. They are very low.

Then the waves get near land. The water is shallow. The waves bunch up. They become higher. They become **dangerous**.

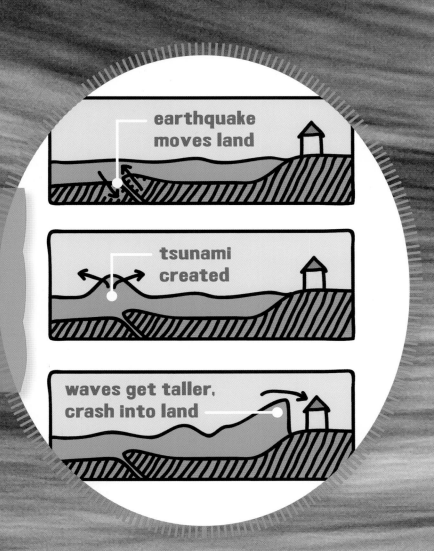

earthquake moves land

tsunami created

waves get taller, crash into land

arrival time

The tides happen regularly. We know when and where tides will happen. It takes about six hours to go from low tide to high tide. So tidal waves are **predictable**.

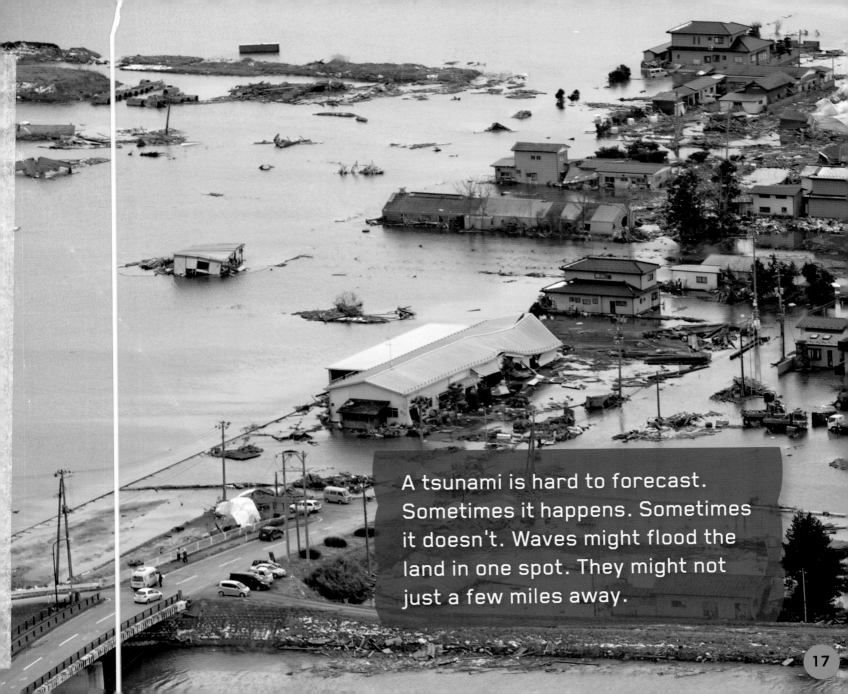

A tsunami is hard to forecast. Sometimes it happens. Sometimes it doesn't. Waves might flood the land in one spot. They might not just a few miles away.

how much damage?

Tidal waves are usually not **dangerous**. People surf on them. Tidal waves aren't **destructive**. Although one might wash your sand castle away!

A tsunami can be very **dangerous**.
The wave rushes over the land.
It knocks trees and buildings
over. It causes a lot of **damage**.

gentle or hard?

A tidal wave is usually gentle. It is fun to play in on the beach.

A tsunami is a certain kind of wave. It can travel a long way. It can be very **destructive**.

at a glance

tidal wave ——————— tsunami

happens in the ocean ——————— happens in the ocean and large lakes and rivers

caused by the moon and sun ——————— caused by sudden movement of land

predictable ——————— happens unexpectedly

usually gentle ——————— usually **destructive**

tidal wave in a pan

make a model of shoreline destruction

after

before

What You'll Need

- paint roller pan
- measuring cup
- sand
- water
- fancy toothpicks
- paper umbrellas
- camera
- small, empty plastic bottle

22

1. Put 5 cups of sand in the pan. Push it to the shallow end. This is the beach.

2. Add 6 cups of water to the deep end. Pour slowly. This is the ocean.

3. Stick toothpicks into the sand. These are trees. Add some paper umbrellas.

4. Take a picture of the beach.

5. Make sure the cap is on the plastic bottle. Lay it in the water.

6. Gently **bob** the bottle up and down. This makes waves.

7. Watch the motion of the waves. Keep bobbing the bottle for 2 minutes.

8. Remove the bottle. Let the water settle. Take another picture of the beach.

think about it

How did the beach change? Why did the toothpicks and umbrellas tip over?

glossary

bob – to move, or cause to move, quickly up and down.

cycle – a series of events that happen over and over again.

damage – harm or ruin.

dangerous – able or likely to cause harm or injury.

destructive – causing damage.

earthquake – when the ground shakes or trembles.

landslide – when a large amount of rocks or dirt slide down a hill.

predictable – able to be seen or learned of before it happens.